IS CHRISTIANITY FOR REAL?

Answers to Five Common Myths about Christianity

MICHAEL GREEN AND GORDON CARKNER

BARBOUR
PUBLISHING, INC.
Uhrichsville, Ohio

Text copyright © 1988 Michael Green and Gordon Carkner. Original edition published in English under the title *Ten Myths about Christianity* by Lion Publishing plc, Oxford, England. Copyright © Lion Publishing, plc 1988.

This edition copyright © 2001 by Barbour Publishing, Inc.

ISBN 1-58660-268-3

All rights reserved. No part of this publication may be reproduced or transmitted in any form or by any means without written permission of the publisher.

Scripture taken from the HOLY BIBLE, NEW INTERNATIONAL VERSION ®. NIV®. Copyright © 1973, 1978, 1984 by International Bible Society. Used by permission of Zondervan Publishing House. All rights reserved.

Published by Barbour Publishing, Inc., P. O. Box 719, Uhrichsville, Ohio 44683 http://www.barbourbooks.com

Printed in the United States of America.

CONTENTS

Introduction 5
Christianity Stifles Personal Freedom . . 10
Christianity Is Just a Crutch
   for the Weak 18
People Become Christians through Social
   Conditioning. 26
Christians Are Otherworldly
   and Irrelevant to Modern Life 34
It Doesn't Matter What You Believe.
   All Religions Are Basically the Same. . . 41

INTRODUCTION

"It was the best of times: It was the worst of times." These words of Charles Dickens to describe the years of the French Revolution fit our own day remarkably well. Yes, it is the best of times: Would you prefer to have lived in any other century? The fantastic advances in science and technology, the control of disease and the length of life, the comfort of homes and the ease of travel in what has become a global village... It would all have been undreamed-of even a hundred years ago.

But it is no less the worst of times. There has never been such a threat to life on this planet as there is today. Never has there been such rape of our world's resources, never such famine, so many deaths by torture. The injustice in society, the breakdown of marriage, the abuse of wives and children, the absence of values, and the inhuman way we treat each other are breathtaking in a world that is consider civilized. The old Russian joke hits close to home: "Under capitalism man exploits man. Under communism the reverse is true"! Underneath all the surface ills of our society there is a profound loss of identity and purpose. Who am I? Where is the world going? What really matters? What will last? The old remedies for the human condition have been found wanting. The optimism of the humanists? Shattered on the rock of two bestial world wars and the continual carnage in world society. Marxism's economic restructuring? Human hearts remain as unfulfilled in China as in Manhattan. Materialism? Utterly selfish and utterly unsatisfying—some of the richest people in the world are the most unhappy. Dr. Ronald Conway, a leading Australian psychiatrist, wrote of Melbourne society what is true of many "first-world" countries: "We have in parts of Melbourne the highest barbiturate dependence in the world, the highest suicide rate among young males between eighteen and thirty, the highest declared rate of rape in the world, and one in four women and one in ten men are suffering from depression. Australians have everything, and yet they have nothing to live for." Where, then, shall we look for an answer to the most profound questions of our lives and our society? Is there any guidance to be had? Are there any values that will last?

During the height of the Roman Empire, at the crossroads of Greek, Roman, and Jewish culture, Jesus of Nazareth was born. His life and teaching, His death and resurrection have captured the hearts and minds of millions all over the world during the past two thousand years, and today a third of the world's population claims to follow Him.

Here was His Manifesto:

"The Spirit of the Lord is on me, because he has anointed me to preach good news to the poor. He has sent me to proclaim freedom for the prisoners and recovery of sight for the blind, to release the oppressed, to proclaim the year of the Lord's favor" (Luke 4:18–19).

He claims that He has come to bring the answer to the human condition, reconcile the estranged, and bring hope to the most despairing. So immensely valuable are we to God that Jesus has come to show us what God is like and to call for our commitment. As we surrender ourselves to that undeserved love, we shall discover what life is all about and what human beings were made for. That is the claim, no less. But is it credible that this individual from two thousand years ago can have anything to say to our modern world? Can today's rootless, emotionally wounded men and women find any reason for hope in Jesus of Nazareth? We believe they can. Many thousands of people every day across the world are entrusting their lives to this Jesus, most in Africa, Asia, and Latin America. Properly understood, and personally trusted, He remains the only hope for mankind.

But the real Jesus, and true Christianity, have been obscured. Myths cluster around Him and His way of life, like barnacles on the bottom of a ship after a long voyage. This book attempts to scrape off the barnacles, to explode the myths, and to enable you to make your considered response to the real Jesus. The five myths we have chosen are not arbitrary. They represent what a great many people think and say. Because they insulate people from the real Jesus, they need to be ripped away. If we are to accept Jesus and Christianity we need to be clear what we are accepting. If we reject Him, we need to be equally clear what it is we are rejecting and why. It is the aim of this little book to make the issues crystal clear.

CHRISTIANITY STIFLES PERSONAL FREEDOM

"Freedom" is the prevailing cry of modern times, at the individual and at the national level. It is also an overwhelming psychological preoccupation in the West.

Yet for so central an idea it has been left curiously undefined. Often freedom is seen very superficially, as the removal of immediate constraints without thinking where this autonomy will all lead. Frequently it leads to abuse. Liberty turns into license and is used for merely selfish ends. Heady wine though it is, freedom can produce some very painful hangovers.

Yet freedom of the right kind is essential for our humanity. So if, as some believe, Christianity stifles our freedom, then it should be raised.

At the same time, it is strange that

Christianity should be thought an enemy of freedom. After all, it is Christianity which has so often stood up for the poor and oppressed, the captive and the underprivileged. Liberation from ignorance, disease, and political subjugation has resulted time and again where Christian faith and principles have been brought to bear. So why should it seem repressive?

Part of the answer lies simply in the selfishness of our hearts. We want our own way. We see God as a celestial policeman, and we want to run away from Him and thumb our noses at His regulations. We want to do our own thing. And it is obvious that allegiance to Jesus Christ will put some limits on this freedom.

Another part is the sad reality of legalistic Christians. A lot of Christians seem to have developed an extensive list of dos and don'ts which seem both stupid and petty. If Christianity means submitting to bourgeois legalism, then no thank you.

But at a deeper level, the answer lies in the wide assumption that there are no standards which have absolute claim on us. Facts are one thing, as many think, such as scientific facts. But values are entirely subjective. You take your pick in the ethical supermarket of life, and you don't complain when others select different values.

"The greatest question of our time is not communism versus individualism; not East versus West; it is whether man can bear to live without God in an age which has killed him." So writes the historian Will Durant. The point is a powerful one. Most people in the Western lands live as if God is dead. If that is so, ethics can only derive from human custom or from personal choice. And therein lies the problem.

As Woody Allen put it in his inimitable way, "More than at any time in history, mankind stands at a crossroad. One path leads to total extinction. Let us pray that we have the wisdom to choose correctly."

Or, in the more prosaic words of the moralist Mark Hanna, "The importance of moral experience can hardly be overestimated, for today the human race stands at the brink of self-destruction. It is not first of all technology but moral decision-making that will determine whether or not we have a future, and if so, what kind of future it will be."

Hanna is right. If morals are simply a matter of headcount, if values are all relative and depend on personal choice, the world is heading for destruction. Dr. Paul Johnson, the British historian, writes, "What is so notable about the twentieth century and a principal cause of its horrors is that great physical power has been acquired by men who have no fear of God and who believe themselves restrained by no absolute code of conduct."

If there are no absolute values, then what

is our basis for distinguishing between Mother Teresa and Adolf Hitler? Why should it be thought better to save the lives of castaways in the streets of Calcutta than to murder six million people in gas chambers? But the moment you admit that one course of action is without qualification better than another, you admit the existence of an absolute standard by which you are judging.

Alexander Solzhenitsyn, in his celebrated address at Harvard, showed how shallow is the popular philosophy of hedonism, having a good time as the goal of life. "If humanism were right in declaring that man is born to be happy, he would not have to die. But since he is born to die, his task on earth must be of a spiritual nature. . .so that one may leave this life a better human being than when he started it."

Freedom, then, must be about more than choosing our code of conduct. It is to do with the kind of people we are. Jesus of Nazareth strikes me as the most liberated man who ever lived. He knew very well there was a divinely appointed standard of ethics, and He framed His life in accordance with it. He said, "I always do what pleases him (God)" (John 8:29). But could anyone say that His faith stifled His freedom? He was utterly free of covetousness, free of hypocrisy, free of the fear of others, free to be Himself. He was free to look into people's hearts and tell them the truth about themselves, free to love men and women with warmth and purity, and free at the end to voluntarily surrender His life for others.

Was there ever so free a human being? Yet He had discovered the truth that freedom is not the license to do what you want but the liberation to do what you ought. He has shown that real freedom is unselfish and warm, generous and person-centered, more to do with relationships than rule keeping. Jesus is the free person's model. Duty did not stifle

Him. Obedience did not obliterate His freedom. Circumstances did not imprison Him. He was utterly free—free to use His power for others, free to love the unlovely, free to confront oppressors and injustice. The ultimate liberated man.

And true Christian freedom is Jesus-shaped. There is no sniff of legalism about it. It is based on the conviction that there is indeed an absolute in the realm of ethics, and that this ideal is not unknown to us. It has been given personal embodiment in Jesus of Nazareth. So Christian freedom is nothing to do with rules and regulations. It is everything to do with pleasing Christ and allowing Him to be the model for our relationships with God and fellow man, for our service of others, for our standards of honesty and purity. It is allowing the best human being who ever lived to be the inspiration for our living. What is stifling about that? To be sure, it may often run against the way of our selfish indulgence, but that is necessary in any pursuit of excellence. It applies to the athlete, the academic, the doctor. Christian freedom stands irrespective of our circumstances. It progressively releases us to be the kind of human being that in our best moments we want to be. And it results in the sort of behavior which, if universalized, would not destroy society but transform it.

In a word, the only freedom which Christianity stifles is the freedom to injure ourselves and other people. True freedom only comes from Jesus.

CHRISTIANITY IS JUST A CRUTCH FOR THE WEAK

Some people pride themselves in their strength. They feel almost invincible. And so they can easily despise a faith that speaks of strengthening the weak and lifting up the fallen.

"I don't need Christianity," they say. "It's just a crutch for the weaklings!"

I have often heard a sneer like that. And I wonder how the young person, full of health and scorn who utters it, would feel if he or she fell downstairs and broke a leg. I guess that person's attitude to crutches might change!

Perhaps we have grown so accustomed to the crutches of our society that we hardly recognize them for what they are. The mad quest for intimacy, to still the ever present pain of loneliness. The activism with which we fill our lives because we dare not stop and ask who we are and where we are going. The dependence on alcohol and drugs because the pressures around and within us have gotten too great. The anxiety state which demands an array of tranquilizers before we can face going to sleep at night. The attempt to prop up our lives with material things. Or the reaction which drives us to Eastern mysticism and seminars for the improvement of our human potential. Crutches, every one of them.

Other props are less obvious but just as much crutches for the weak: power over other people, fame, wealth, beauty. There seems no end to the props people use as they go limping through life.

And Christianity—is it just another crutch?

In one sense, yes it is. Christianity is for people who do not pretend they are invincible but know they have something broken. If ours were a perfect world and we were perfect people there might be no need for

Christianity. But such is not the case. Our world, our lives are fractured by greed and lust, by cruelty and selfishness. Don't believe me? Just glance at a newspaper or watch the television news.

Christianity is unashamedly a rescue religion. That is why so many self-satisfied people steer clear of it. "It is not the healthy who need a doctor," said Jesus, "but the sick" (see Matthew 9:12). But He knew that in His meaning no one is healthy. Not even you or me.

As George Orwell put it tartly in *Nineteen Eighty Four,* "We have found the enemy: it is us." But most of us won't even admit our injuries, obvious though they are to everybody else. Unless we do, we shall have to continue to hobble through life. Our makeshift crutches will not bear our weight. We need radical healing. And that is precisely what Jesus Christ offers.

Set side by side two estimates of human nature. We think we have hearts of gold. But the prophet Jeremiah said, "The heart is deceitful above all things and beyond cure" (Jeremiah 17:9). Which evaluation is closer to the mark?

Think how often in the course of the day our words let us down: bitter words, hasty words, filthy words, cruel words, lying words. Think how often we have reason to be ashamed of our actions: greedy, unfair, self-centered, thoughtless, cruel actions, very often. And how about our characters? I wonder how those who work with us and under us would assess those? As for our thoughts—which of us would not blush to the roots of our hair if our thoughts could be flashed onto a television screen for all to see?

How does God react to all this? By pretending it does not matter? Of course it matters. The evil in our lives spoils our character, it ruins relationships, and it alienates us from Him. Moreover it has an uncanny grip on us. Which of us does not long to be free of the moral weakness which pulls us down?

The Christian good news is that God has acted to restore the situation. He has come to this world to show us what He is really like, to show us how we could live life at its best.

But that isn't all. He came to build a bridge over the troubled waters of our alienation and selfishness. He came to construct a road back to God. And He did this, against all human logic, by laying down His life for us. Our wickedness had erected an impenetrable barrier between us and God. When Jesus died on the cross He broke through the barrier, even though its masonry fell on Him and killed Him. He picked up the tab for our debts, all of us. He took responsibility for the evil and wickedness of the whole wide world, drained its poison, and wiped the slate clean. And He could do so, fittingly, because He was God as well as man. "God was reconciling the world to himself in Christ" (2 Corinthians 5:19). And because He did so each of us can face God with an uncondemning conscience, our debts paid.

What is more, even death could not hold Jesus down. He rose again on the first Easter Day. He is alive, and Christians claim not just to know about Him but to know Him in a personal encounter. They are convinced that this risen Christ gives them the power to overcome habits which previously had pulled them down time after time.

It is, therefore, a radical reshaping of human nature that Christianity offers. It liberates us from the shackles of the past, and sets us free to be the people we were intended to be. It enables us to make the contribution toward other people and society at large which we know to be right, but which, because of our unhealed self-centeredness, we never actually got around to.

I suppose you could say that the wood of the cross is like a splint for our fractured lives. But that splint is applied with the intention of effecting a cure, to enable us to stand and walk and run.

See what happens to some of the "weak" who avail themselves of this "crutch."

- A Mother Teresa comes out of her nunnery to love the helpless and homeless on the streets of Calcutta.
- A David Sheppard, international athlete with a glittering future, gives his life to serve the needs of the inner city, first as clergyman then as bishop.
- A Chuck Colson, ruthless self-seeking lawyer and presidential aide who had a share in the guilt of Watergate, gives the rest of his life to seeking social and political justice in the name of Christ and ministering to the needs of prisoners.
- A George Foreman, former heavyweight boxing champion of the world, whose scarred face is now full of the love of Christ, might mutter gently in your ear, "What was that I heard you say—that Christianity is a crutch for the weak?"

- An Alexander Solzhenitsyn, rotting in the Gulag and surrendering his whole intellect and being to the Jesus who lived and died and rose for him, gains the strength to challenge a totalitarian regime on behalf of human dignity and freedom.

And those are just samples from the millions who have thrown away the pathetic crutches with which they used to limp along the road of life. They have come for healing to the seasoned wood of the cross, and they have been transformed.

If you think Christianity is a crutch for the weak, make sure that your accusation is not a smokescreen to deny your own inadequacies. Make sure that it is not an excuse to evade the claims that the living God has on your life. His remedy is very radical, but very effective. He takes wounded, fractured people and makes them whole.

PEOPLE BECOME CHRISTIANS THROUGH SOCIAL CONDITIONING

Only a fool would claim that cultural circumstances play no part at all in people's religious beliefs.

We are all affected greatly by our heredity and our environment, and particularly by friends whose opinions we value. Nobody would deny that a Hindu environment predisposes you toward Hinduism, a Christian one to Christianity and so forth. But the question is, do heredity and environment constitute a complete explanation of why people believe and behave as they do? That is altogether more questionable.

A "Christian" background may put you off to Christianity. A great many children in Sunday schools revolt by the age of eleven, and sometimes children of clergy families determine in their teens to have nothing more to do with organized religion. How does this fact, and fact it is, square with the assertion that conversion and religious experience are the result, and only the result, of social conditioning?

More often still, it works the other way. Many millions of people in China these days are becoming Christians, in the teeth of sustained opposition by the authorities. Prisons around the world are full of Christians who are certainly not there because they are socially conditioned toward the faith. Everything in their environment inclines them in the direction of atheism and dialectical materialism. Yet Communism and other anti-Christian philosophies have been totally unable to stop the growth of Christian conversions in these lands. Interesting, isn't it? Great revivals of Christianity have taken place in strictly communist countries of the world. Who is going to tell me that this is due to social conditioning?

Perhaps even more impressive are the Sawi tribespeople whom Don Richardson, a pioneer missionary, describes in his *Peace Child*. Their culture was so corrupt that every single human virtue was deemed a vice among them, and deception was thought the highest virtue. When they heard the story of Jesus for the first time they cheered the treachery of Judas Iscariot. He was the hero! There is a very flourishing Christian community there now. Social conditioning? Tell me another!

This same argument about social conditioning is regularly applied to conscience. So far from supplying a categorical imperative in our lives, telling us which is the right way to go, conscience is seen by atheist philosophers as merely the reflection of social pressures on us. Naturally, conscience is affected to some extent by the society in which we live, but that cannot be a full explanation. Most of the moral advances in history have been brought about by passionate reformers who stood out boldly against the pressures of their society because of what their conscience told them was right. Think of the liberation of slaves, of women, of children condemned to fifteen hours a day in the factories, or prisoners chained day and night to the walls of their cells. In every case reform was brought about on strictly conscientious grounds, and in every case in the teeth of the opposition of society and its standards at the time. Conscience is no product of social conditioning.

But if social reasons lie behind what some people believe, then they explain atheism as well as other creeds. Paul Vitz, a noted Christian psychologist, was brought up as a Christian. Then at eighteen he abandoned his heritage and became an atheist. At thirty-eight, by now a professor of psychology, he reinvestigated Christianity, came to the conclusion it was true, and committed his life to Christ. He now declares that his reasons for adopting atheism were "superficial, irrational, and largely without intellectual and moral integrity." He did it in order to win favor with his peers.

Christian conversion is much misunderstood. It is regarded as sudden, irrational, selective, if not downright illusory. But what are its essential elements?

They may perhaps best be seen in the archetype of all Christian conversions, that of Saul of Tarsus. While much of the paraphernalia of his conversion was unique, four elements stand out which are present in every authentic conversion.

- It touched his conscience. He knew that he was kicking against the goads (Acts 26:14).
- It touched his understanding. He realized that the Jesus he was persecuting was the risen Messiah and Son of God.
- It touched his will. He came to the point of giving in to Jesus and beginning to follow Him.

- It changed his whole life—his ambitions, his character, his relationships, his whole perspective on life. No conversion can claim to be real unless it embodies these four elements.

But what if the whole thing is an illusion? What if Freud was right in regarding religious experience itself as illusory? There are, I believe, three tests which it is proper to apply if you are wondering whether religious experience in general and Christianity in particular is illusory.

First, the test of history. This does not apply to all religions, only to those that make historical claims. But it is most certainly the case with Christianity. It revolves entirely around the person and death and resurrection of Jesus of Nazareth, a carpenter-teacher who lived under Roman occupation of Palestine in the first third of the first century A.D. There is nothing illusory about Jesus, nor is there in the impact He had on His contemporaries in all subsequent generations the world over. His life of love and integrity, or courage and insight is unparalleled. There is nothing illusory about His claims. His death was real enough and widely witnessed. And His resurrection is extremely well attested. Nor could anyone doubt the reality of the church that has sprung from Jesus and now claims many millions of adherents throughout the world. It simply makes no sense to argue that Christian faith is illusory, the product of social conditioning. It is rooted in history. Its founder and origins will survive the most searching scrutiny.

Second, there is the test of character. When drunkards become sober and crooks become honest, when animists lose their bondage to the spirit world and people enslaved by black magic are set free, when self-centered people become generous—well, it is very difficult to put the reason for all this down to illusion. The transformation of people's lives is not the only criterion of authenticity, but it has been very impressive among Christians down the centuries.

Third, there is the test of power. That is another criterion of the validity of religious experience. All that we know about delusions and obsessional neuroses is that they tend toward the disintegration of character, unbalanced behavior, and the inability to achieve goals. But Christianity has precisely the opposite effect. It makes people whole. And its power continues through life and in the face of death—when many delusions are stripped away.

None of these three tests is attribual to social conditioning. The social-conditioning theory cannot explain historical facts or the deep change in people's characters. As an explanation of the power of Christianity it will not do.

CHRISTIANS ARE OTHERWORLDLY AND IRRELEVANT TO MODERN LIFE

This is often said but hard to understand. Most Christians today could do with being more concerned with the hereafter, not less. In a previous generation heaven and hell loomed large in the minds of believers, but today many professing Christians seem rather less preoccupied with life after death.

This is a pity, because history shows that the people who have done most for this world are those who have been most sure about the next. Think of Augustine, who sat down as the barbarians were surging like a rising tide into the Roman Empire, and wrote a book called *The City of God* which inspired leading thinkers for the next thousand years.

Reformers such as Luther and Calvin had their heads in heaven, you might think. But the effects on earth shook the whole of Europe.

If your horizon is bounded by this world, you have no star to steer by. You cannot reach beyond your very circumscribed personal world to find any larger perspective. But if you believe in the living God, who made this world but is not bound by it, then your outlook changes radically. You see history as moving toward a goal. You gain some glimpse of the ideal by which this world can be judged and toward which you can see to move society. The coming of Jesus links this world to the next. He is the kingdom of God in person. And as people are committed to Him, so they enlist in the furthering of that kingdom on earth. There is no romantic idealism about this. People are sick of utopias which disappoint (the literal meaning of the Greek word utopia is "nowhere-land").

What Christians are concerned with is highly relevant to this world and its needs, for the very simple reason that they know God shares that concern. He proved it by coming in Jesus, dying for us, and rising from the tomb on the first Easter Day. God could not have done more to show He is involved, up to the neck. And so Christians, in their turn, are committed to getting involved in bringing the values and standards, the love and concerns, the justice and truthfulness of the Age to Come into this here and now. They know it will never be complete. There is no starry-eyed idealism about them. They see themselves as an embassy of heaven, living out the life of their parent state in a foreign land whose good they seek to promote. Perhaps only otherworldly people can really do much earthly good.

But if Christians today could use a bit more otherworldliness, their faith is certainly not irrelevant.

If ever there was a need for Christian values and motivation, surely it is now. The perils of a world where the doom clock points at six minutes to midnight; the carnage in scores of conflicts all over the globe; the decimation wrought by famine of unimagined proportions; the social violence; the disregard of the individual; the widespread oppression—all these things make the need for Christian involvement greater than ever before. Do we not need the Christian charities to respond to the natural disasters in the world? Do we not need the Tutus and the Solzhenitsyns to plead the cause of justice in countries like South Africa and the Soviet Union? And who is going to do it unless it is those who have some Archimedean point outside their own society from which to speak in the name of truth, compassion, and justice? Why is it that Christian doctors can serve in the most primitive situations, where others without a Christian faith are not found?

Once you are captivated by the self-sacrifice of Jesus, you cannot insulate yourself from the world of need He came to minister to. If you believe that human beings really matter, as children of God, then you are simply bound to get involved with them for their welfare.

"It is a serious thing", wrote C. S. Lewis, "to live in a society of potential gods and goddesses... It is immortals whom we joke with, work with, marry, snub, exploit—immortal horrors or everlasting splendors."

That is the logic behind Christian social involvement. And whenever the tide of faith sweeps in, there is always a corresponding rise in social concern and service to the community, as happened in England in the nineteenth century. Almost every aspect of social reform was brought about, not by the agnostic followers of John Stuart Mill, but by men and women brought to a living faith through the revivals that had so profoundly affected the country. The Great Reform Bill was brought in largely through the influence of Christian parliamentarians. The Earl of Shaftesbury was responsible for the Mines Act, forbidding women and children to be forced to work down the mines, the Factories Act limiting hours of work, and so forth. Dr. Barnardo founded homes for orphans. Elizabeth Fry brought about prison reform. Josephine Butler got Parliament to outlaw child prostitution and protect women. And of course Wilberforce, a little earlier, had lived to see his lifelong struggle for the abolition of slavery crowned with success.

All these people acted so effectively and passionately in this world because they were so clear about the next. They had come to a living faith in Christ, and because of it they were strengthened to serve Him in practical ways for the good of others whom He had made. The same is true of men like Martin Luther King Jr., Mother Teresa, and a horde of others in our own day.

All of them were persuaded that the atheist account of the world was profoundly wrong. We are not, as Jean-Paul Sartre maintained, "an empty bubble on the sea of nothingness." If you believe that, then there is no good reason to put yourself out for other people. But if you believe we are made in the image of God, so valuable that Christ died for us, then you roll up your sleeves and get involved. That is what real Christianity requires. And that is what Christians at their best have always done.

IT DOESN'T MATTER WHAT YOU BELIEVE. ALL RELIGIONS ARE BASICALLY THE SAME.

Of all the myths we have examined this seems the most charitable and sensible. It accords with the tolerance which is one of the virtues we cherish most. But on closer inspection it proves highly unsatisfactory.

In no other realm of life would we apply such an argument. What teacher would be satisfied with pupils who said, "It does not matter what answer you give in algebra, Latin, history, or geography. It all comes to the same thing in the end"? We may have multiple-choice questions today, but multiple answers? In religion as in everything else, we are called to judge which answers fit the facts.

Is it really likely that all religions lead to

God, when they are so different, indeed so contradictory? In Hinduism the divine is plural and impersonal; The God of Islam is singular and personal; the God of Christianity is the creator of the world; the divine of Buddhism is neither personal nor creative. You could scarcely have a greater contrast than that. Christianity teaches that God both forgives and assists us; in Buddhism there is no possibility of forgiveness and no hope of supernatural aid. The goal of all existence is *nirvana,* extinction, attained by the Buddha after no less than 547 births; the goal of all existence in Christianity is to know God and to enjoy Him forever. The use of images figures prominently in Hinduism; Judaism prohibits making any image of God. Islam allows a man four wives; Christianity one. Perhaps the greatest difference of all lies between the Bible which asserts that we can never save ourselves, try as we will; and all the other faiths which assert that a person will be saved, or reborn, or made whole, or achieve fulfillment by keeping teachings or living according to laws.

Nothing spells out this contrast more powerfully than comparing a Buddhist story with the very similar parable of the prodigal son. In both, a boy comes home and is met by his father. But where the prodigal son is met with quite undeserved forgiveness and welcome, the Buddhist equivalent has to work off the penalty for his past misdeeds by years of servitude.

It does religion no service to pretend that all faiths are the same beneath some superficial clothing. They are not. They lead to radically different goals. Extinction or heaven; pardon or paying it off; a personal God or an impersonal monad; salvation by grace or by works. The contrasts are irreconcilable.

Then why are so many people dedicated to such a shaky proposition?

- For several interesting reasons, the

world has become a global village. Various faiths jostle one another just as various nationalities bump into one another in the streets. It is tacitly assumed that racial pluralism validates religious pluralism. But it is a myth.

- Tolerance has reached such a stage that we assume God is a good, genial fellow. He will not blame us for our faults. Nobody could possibly be lost. But that too is a myth.
- Many act today as though faith in itself is what really matters. You have to believe in something, but it does not really matter what. That is another myth. Faith is like a rope. It matters enormously what you attach it to.
- And also, this approach means people can avoid decision. If all religions are the same, we don't have to choose. We'll be all right anyhow. But will we? What if that is another myth?

This easy assumption, that we are all looking for God and will all find Him in the end, is false both to what God is like and to human nature. If there is a God at all, then He is the source of ourselves and of our environment. He is Lord over all life. How can we puny human beings climb up to Him? How can we comprehend Him? Obviously, we can't. The only hope is that He may have somewhere shown us what He is like. The Bible, and only the Bible, claims that such a revelation has happened. Dimly at first, then with increasing light in the Old Testament, people began to see the truth of a God who loves us and speaks to us. Then the stage was set for God's final and decisive self-disclosure, in the coming of His Son. No longer is He the unknown God. "No one has ever seen God, but God the one and only, who is at the Father's side, has made him known" (John 1:18).

If the nature of God is one reason why

the creature can never find his way to the creator unaided, human nature is the other. The Bible tells us that we are essentially selfish, that we do not follow every gleam of light when we get it, but on the contrary we frequently turn our back on the light and try to extinguish it. It tells us that there is a basic twist in human nature that makes us go wrong without our really trying.

If this is so, then we have no prospect of reaching God, and no religion can span the gulf between a holy God and us in our sinfulness. If there is to be any hope for us, there must be a divine rescue. Not only must God show us what He is like, but He must also find a way to bring rebels back into His family, to reconcile enemies who want only to go their own way. The Bible, and the Bible alone, tells us that there is such a God and that He has found a way. The cross is the way by which God can justly forgive our sins and frailties: He has himself paid the penalty (1 Peter 2:24).

So you see Christianity is not really a religion at all, if by "religion" you mean a way of trying to find God. It is a revelation and a rescue.

- It is a revelation of what God is like; and it comes in a form we can really take in, the form of a human life. It is also a revelation of what we are like, for men and women could not bear the purity of that life of Jesus but hounded Him to the cross.
- It is also a rescue. God came to find me. And He met me in the death of His Son and beside the empty tomb from which His Son rose victorious.

Most amazing of all, this God, who provides both a revelation and a rescue instead of a religion, wants to meet me. He wants to relate to me in a personal way which even death will not be able to sever. No faith in the world is remotely comparable to this. All religions are not basically the same. It does matter very much what you believe.

Does this mean that all other religions are totally wrong? Of course not. All have some measure of truth in them; the highest ones such as Islam and Judaism have a great deal of truth in them. They are like varied candles and lights in the darkness of the world. But they all pale into insignificance at the dawn. And the dawn has come with Jesus Christ. He fulfills the hopes and aspirations, the virtues and insights of whatever is true and good in all faiths.